I dedicate this book to first of all to my Lord and Savior Christ Jesus... my example, my friend, my advisor, and my... everything...

My children...thank you for being my laughter and my joy.

Zhaquita

Jacob

Chontis

Jannis

....each of my grandchildren...Grand Mimi loves you...

To that person that looks into the Fathers heart and encourages us to worship during devotional services…

To everyone that truly aspire to know and love the Lord more

and more.

All the people that labor interpreting and ministering within the deaf ministries …God will not forget your labor of love…

Table of Contents

Preface …

This book was written to encourage a way of worshipping by using sign language. My aim is to worship God with all of my might and with all of the skills that God gave me. I also desire for all to enjoy God's presence.

What you are about to read is solely my experiences and do not reflect the only way nor is it a case study.

For those of you that have not worshiped the Lord…Oh my…you must.

We were created to worship God Almighty,

...John 4:23 ...But the hour cometh, and now is, when the true worshippers shall worship the Father in spirit and in truth: for the Father seeketh such to worship Him...KJV

God desired our company ...so much that He made a way for [humankind] us to be in His presence again, for the man that He created made a decision that caused the fellowship with them to be broken. [Disobeying God's ways and commands which is called sin]

...1 Cor 15:22...For as in Adam all die, even so in Christ shall all be made alive...KJV

Man has a free will to choose God or not, God always made sure that there was a way for the people He created to have access back to Him. The sin that was welcomed into this world by Adam, the first man kept us from getting too close. God is a Holy God. Any sin that comes before Him would be destroyed. Therefore, anyone with sin that try to be in God's presence would die.

...John 3:16... For God so loved the world that he gave his only begotten Son, that whosoever believeth in Him should not perish, but have everlasting life...KJV

God loved us and desired us so much that He sent His son to die with the sin placed on Him…for us, instead of us.

Now, we can have this gift of eternal life by receiving His Son into our hearts. For this Son, Jesus, also rose from the dead and ascended into heaven for us to have fellowship with the Creator again.

His Spirit manifests as we worship Him.

...Luke 10:27... Thou shall love the Lord thy God with all thy heart, and with all thy soul and with all thy strength, and with all thy mind...KJV

Ischus 1. Ability, force, strength, might

If you never received Jesus into your heart, you may do that now...

Jesus...I desire to have you as Lord and Savior over my life.

I know that you died for my sins, I repent of my sins [meaning; I turn from wanting to sin and turn towards your guidance in life].

Thank you for dying for my sins. Cleanse me from every one of them.

Thank you also for raising again from the dead that I may have new life through you…

Lead me each day and I will follow your word.

Thank you for saving me.

In Jesus name I pray

Amen

…Wonderful! … Now you can worship God and experience the manifestation of God's Holy Spirit.

Receive Him

Let's start…

Know the difference between worshipping and praising God. When we praise God, we are thinking on various things that He did in our lives, from the little to the large things.

…Psalms 150:2… Praise him for his mighty acts: praise him according to his excellent greatness…KJV

When we worship God, we are "loving" Him and thanking Him for just being who He is…

Psalms 95:6... O come, lets worship and bow down: let us kneel before the Lord our maker...KJV

...Phil 3:3... For we are the circumcision, which worship God in the spirit, and rejoice in Christ Jesus, and have no confidence in the fresh...KJV

Some people are aware of how to praise God and do this when good things are happening in their lives. Some people have learned that they could praise Him in advance, for what He will be doing in their lives.

This is needed...for God is worthy of our praises. However, imagine if the only praise we received was due to an action we have done and other times we would barely be acknowledged.

How would we feel?

Would we feel slighted?

Now imagine if someone wanted just to be with us without wanting something from us.

...Luke 7:36-39, 44-47...And one of the Pharisees desired him that he would eat with him. And he went into the Pharisee's house, and sat down to meat. And, behold, a woman in the city, which was a sinner, when she knew that Jesus sat at meat in the Pharisee's house, brought an alabaster box of ointment. And stood at his feet behind him weeping, and began to wash his feet with tears, and did wipe them with the hairs of her head, and kissed his feet, and anointed them with the ointment. Now when the Pharisee which had bidden him saw it, he spake within himself, saying, This man, if he were a prophet, would have known who and what manner of woman this is that touched him: for she is a sinner...KJV

...44... And he turned to the woman, and said unto Simon, Seest thou this woman? I entered into thine house, thou gavest me no water for my feet; but she hath washed my feet with tears, and wiped them with the hairs of her head. Thou gavest me no kiss: but this woman since the time I came in hath not ceased to kiss my feet. My head with oil thou didst not anoint: but this woman hath anointed my feet with ointment, wherefore I say unto thee, her sins, which are many, are forgiven; for she loved much: but to whom little is forgiven, the same loveth little...KJV

Wouldn't we give gifts and favor to such a person?

...Luke 10:38-42...Now it came to pass, as they went, that he entered into a certain village: and a certain woman named Martha received him into her house. And she had a sister called Mary, which also sat at Jesus' feet, and heard his word. But Martha was cumbered about much serving, and came to him, and said, Lord, dost thou not care that my sister hath left me to serve alone? Bid her therefore that she help me.

And Jesus answered and said unto her. Martha, Martha, thou art careful and troubled about many things: But one thing is needful: And Mary hath chosen that good part, which shall not be taken from her....KJV

God Desires worship from us where we would want to be in His presence and company only because we desire His Spirit.

Lord just because who you are I give you Glory

All Majesty is yours

There is no one like you

Hallelujah!

Hallelujah!

I owe you all my praise

Thank you Jesus for what you have done

And what you are doing

I love you Lord!!!

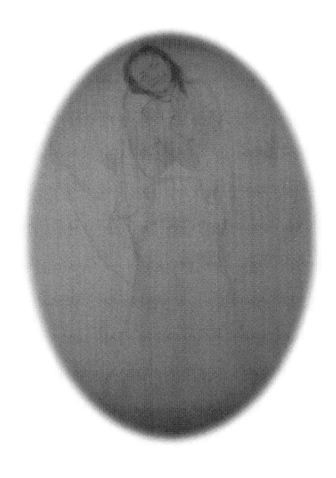

My testimony…

During one time of worship, I was in service on one New Year's Day.

Everyone was praising and worshipping God. I was as well. My Pastor at that time then called for everyone to line up in the middle aisle to be anointed, He prayed for each person that was on line.

I eagerly waited for my turn. What would I receive for the New Year?

My eyes were closed, as I usually do this to prevent visual distractions. When it was my turn to be prayed for, my body relaxed. My knees gave as ushers gently allow my body to lie on the carpet.

To relax physically in the Lord is not rare.

See the scriptures

...John 18: 4-8... Jesus therefore, knowing all things that should come upon him, went forth, and said unto them, whom seek ye? They answered him, Jesus of Nazareth, Jesus saith unto them, I AM he. And Judas also, which betrayed him, stood with them, as soon then as he had said unto them, I am he, they went backward, and fell to the ground. Then asked he them again, whom seek ye? And they said, Jesus of Nazareth. Jesus answered, I have told you that I am he: if therefore ye seek me, let these go their way...KJV as I was there, on the floor, I heard everything that was happening around me and I had the opportunity to get up a I usually acquainted to doing. However, I opted to stay and receive more.

I wanted more from my Heavenly Father. At that time I saw a light [my eyes were closed] that light was bright yet soft.

...John 8:12... Then spake Jesus again unto them, saying, I am the light of the world: he that followeth me shall not walk in darkness, but shall have the light of life...KJV

I then heard the gentle voice of God saying, "I will give you a glimpse of My Glory". At that time, I saw from behind, the robe of God passing by me then that vision was gone.

Though that was a brief span of time, I experience the love of God through this occurrence the love was Holy, absent of fear, full of peace and full of joy.

God allowed me to feel that love. I knew that all the love that I ever knew could not even come close to that love.

When I got up, I carried the remembrance of that love from that time onward. Some things occurred in my life later that showed me why God allowed me to experience this.

I would have never made it without His love.

Therefore, I do not want you, my reader, to be discourage because you did not experience what I did. The trials that I had after I saw that vision were intense. I wouldn't have wanted to continue to live if I have wanted to continue to live if I had not encountered His love,

That love that flowed within my spirit urged me to press towards all He has for me and to share what I have experience.

I am sharing my experience to exhort you to worship God.

Press to worship even more than you are accustom to doing. Again I express what I experience is not exclusively the only way to worship.

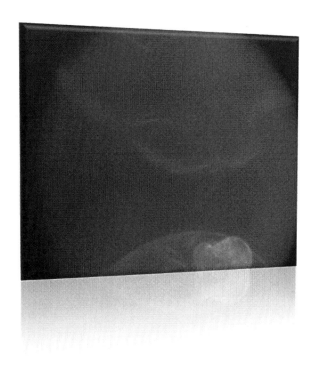

Holy of Holies…

We can lift our hands and praise the Lord freely. We could not do this before. The way is open now for us to enter into God's presence. We now can enter into the Holy of Holies.

This privilege was given because Jesus opened the way up for us to have assessed to the existence of God.

Previously in the Temple of God, the high priest only would be able to enter after first sacrificing a lamb or dove to atone for their sins; then and only then was the high priest able to enter and experience the manifestation of God.

Now we have that access through Jesus [being the final sacrifice needed…the Lamb of God] in which we may enter into the 'Holy God Holies' within us. This is awesome!!!

Now we are not limited to standing outside of the temple gates and hope that God except our sacrifice. Jesus, the Lamb of God which takes away the sins of the world, enable us to be free!!!

We now can worship anywhere, anytime, alone or corporately.

The places of worship could be outdoors, on a train, at work, at home as well as a church building. It is a shame that we do not do it as often as we should.

Of course, in these places other than the use of church, movement and sound is limited for the consideration of the neighbors and people close by.

In church, there is a corporate blessing through worship as a group and usually there is no one there to disturb the vocalized worship.

We have talked about worshipping. All the reasons why and what could happen in the mist of …let's worship

You can close your eyes for less distraction…

Begin with your mouth or with your hands to say thank you Jesus.

As you focus and speak the words of praise and adoration, felt within is God's presence and His presence is sensed in the room of the worshipper.

Hallelujah!!!

Hallelujah!!!

Glory to God!

Lord I praise you and lift your praise up towards heaven thank you Lord, thank you Jesus, thank you!

This is where sign language comes in

...Romans 12:1...I appeal to you therefore, brethren, and beg of you in view of (all) the mercies of God. To make a decisive dedication of your bodies (presenting all your members and faculties) as a living sacrifice, holy (devoted, consecrated) and well pleasing to God, which is your reasonable (rational intelligent) service and spiritual worship...AMP

I have started learning sign language in 1993...an urge to learn sign language developed after I purchased a sign language dictionary.

God gave me a desire to learn more and more words. I then placed these words within songs. This would help me to retain the word into memory.

Many of the words in sign are expressive and can be used within dancing.

My church enabled me to express myself though signing in songs and worship and at times people in the congregation joined in!

Many hearing people find that sign language is a Beautiful language. I thank the deaf community for allowing a hearing person as myself to use their native language.

For God knows sign language and looks forward to my signing to him.

The anointing of God comes on me and causes me to sign better than ever and when that occurs the living word goes through my hands to touch the hearts of people whether deaf or hearing.

I am looking forward to the next time I can express my gratitude to the Lord and to speak with him in prayer using sign language,

It is awesome!!!

Prelude…

I look forward to a time when people whether deaf or hearing will have more of an understanding of the presence of God and enter in Him.

Ephesians 1:16- 23…Cease not to give thanks for you, making mention of you in my prayers. That the God of our Lord Jesus Christ, the Father of Glory, may give unto you the spirit of wisdom and revelation in the knowledge of Him: the eyes of your understanding being enlightened; that ye may know what is the

hope of his calling, and what the riches of glory of his inheritance in the saints, And what is the exceeding greatness of His power to us-ward who believe, according to the working of His mighty power, which He wrought in Christ, when He raised Him from the dead, and set Him to His own right hand in the heavenly places. Far above all principality, and power, might, and dominion, and every name that is named, not only in this world, but also in that which is to come: and hath put all things under His feet, and gave Him to be the head over all things to the church, which is the Body, the fullness of Him that filleth all in all. ..KJV

My other desire is a time when the hearing person will be able to explain to a deaf person what is going on in the service (not only by the interpreter signing)

What I pray is for people becoming saved, delivered, and empowered.

My hope is that you the reader whether you are deaf or hearing have this desire as well and will seek to be an example on how to worship God that everyone may 'hear' (spiritually) the voice of God.

Amen

32030676R00022

Printed in Great Britain
by Amazon